images of Dubai

and the UNITED ARAB EMIRATES

Front cover photographs
Version 1 Burj Al Arab – Jumeirah International (Richard Allenby-Pratt)
Version 2 Emirates Towers – Jumeirah International (Katarina Premfors)

Back cover photograph
Traditional Dhow – Dubai International Marine Beach Club

Text
Christopher Brown

Images of Dubai and the United Arab Emirates
First edition February 2002
Reprint December 2002
Third printing September 2003

Published By
Explorer Publishing & Distribution
Dubai Media City
PO Box 34275, Dubai, UAE
Phone (+971 4) 391 8060
Fax (+971 4) 391 8062
Email: Info@Explorer-Publishing.com
Web: www.Explorer-Publishing.com

ISBN 976-8182-22-9

Text © Explorer Publishing & Distribution 2002
Photographs © photographers as indicated 2002

Colour separations – Gulf Scan
Printing – Emirates Printing Press

images of
Dubai
and the UNITED ARAB EMIRATES

Many a child has dreamt of sailing the seven seas with old Sinbad. For most, our maritime skills – to say nothing of our resolution – prove rather lacking. Quite simply, life tends to get in the way of our adventures. Yet fortune smiles on some of us: those who have stumbled across a different set of seven, the astounding seven emirates of the United Arab Emirates. They comprise a world of adventures, excitement, and exotic beauty packed into a single nation. Although the seven emirates occupy a modest area of 83,600 square kilometers – about the area of Scotland – the historical, cultural, and geographic richness of this nation provides a staggering array of excitement. Piled on top of these delights is the climate: nearly constant sunshine and warmth provide the glorious illusion of an endless summer. Turquoise waters, soft beaches, rugged mountains, vibrant cities, majestic dunes, modern conveniences, and so much more, all bask in the ubiquitous golden yellow sunlight. This book is an attempt to capture – or recapture if you are already familiar with the UAE – some of the dazzling beauty of this corner of Arabia.

For many millennia, Arabia has been a crossroads of cultures, where people, ideas and goods have passed through but left their mark. Beneath the postmodern façade, clear traces of this ancient legacy await discovery. What once was a trade in pearls may now be e-commerce, but the soul and spirit of this nation remain much unchanged. Camels have morphed into luxury cars, burquas into designer sheilahs, yet these are but cosmetic changes to a culture that has proven itself highly adept at adaptation. Throughout the centuries, Arabia has accommodated all manner of changes without losing its identity; why should the discovery of oil be particularly different?

The modern United Arab Emirates fascinates for its graceful balance of cultural history and modern progress. Late in the nineteenth century, the region began its ascent towards modernity: British shipping firms established the port of Dubai as a convenient stopover on the maritime trade route to and from India. This modest start put Dubai on European maps. Early in the twentieth century, the pace of growth and development increased markedly. Quick to recognize the great potential of Dubai as a commercial hub, Sheikh Maktoum Bin Hasher Al Maktoum encouraged development of the Creek and granted a host of tax concessions to traders. The policy proved a great success, and was continued by his successor Sheikh Rashid Bin Saeed Al Maktoum. The arrangement endeared Dubai to the British, and one of the side effects of ensuring their trade and colonial interests was to grant the Trucial States, as the Emirates were known in those days, the status of protectorate. This insulated the region somewhat from other colonial powers and fostered a climate of development and modernization. When the British withdrew from the region in 1971, the United Arab Emirates was poised to begin its meteoric rise into the global community: it had oil, enlightened leadership, and the will to pursue monumental dreams.

In a single generation, the country moved from a loose confederation of tribes to a stable and unified nation. Since 1972, when Ras Al Khaimah joined the nation to complete the unification, the UAE has moved swiftly and decisively towards being a model of peace and prosperity. Growth and development have increased exponentially alongside the burgeoning gross domestic product. Under the leadership of President His Highness Sheikh Zayed Bin Sultan Al Nahyan, the nation finds

Modeled after modern international cities, the major urban centers of the UAE, and particularly Dubai, are emerging as among the most architecturally vibrant places in the world. Funded by huge development budgets, world class architects have been commissioned to experiment with steel, glass, concrete and stone to create enormous sculptures in which people work, live, and play. Not wishing to ignore Arabian history, planning commissions throughout the nation have made a concerted effort to encourage architects and designers to integrate elements of traditional Islamic architecture into all developments. Interlaced patterns and filigree designs, arches and minarets appear in the most unexpected places, and each is a gentle nod to the region's past.

Arabia is often imagined mostly as a desert, but much of the Emirates is far from deserted. Dubai, Abu Dhabi, and Sharjah seem to have sprung out of nowhere, complete neighborhoods appearing in a matter of months. The juxtaposition of worldly cities and unspoiled nature can seem eerie at times. Driving out of Dubai feels at first like crossing a sprawling suburbia, but at a certain point, everything stops and the road carries on into the desert. In equal measure, the cities of the Emirates recall Las Vegas with its incessant recreation of elsewhere. In Dubai one can dine in an Egyptian pyramid; in Abu Dhabi one might rollerblade around a mock volcano; in Sharjah one can entertain fantasies of Venice, and so forth.

Yet these cities are very real. Look closely at the reflections in gleaming glass, or the contrast between neighborhood mosques and multi-national corporate towers, and see a magical place. Buzzing with life and activity, these restless cities allow endless opportunities for work, domesticity, or play. The UAE certainly deserves great praise for its willingness to experiment with various forms of urban development. New malls appear as if by magic on a regular basis, the grand beach resorts of Jumeira feel like tropical islands, and handsome villas of every architectural style sprout in each district.

Dubai feels flashy and quixotic with its endless diversity of size, shape and design. Streets twist and turn along the Creek; dense clusters of skyscrapers rise above neighborhoods of villas; the magnificent row of structures on Sheikh Zayed Road proudly competes with the finest skylines on the globe. Yet equally important to the cityscapes of the UAE are the historical buildings and traditional structures. From nearly any point in the city, a minaret can be seen in some direction. Wind towers and domes appear comfortable next to tower blocks. And public sculpture, gardens, and other art forms prevent a claustrophobic feeling, a pitfall of many other modern cities.

From any high vantage point, the cityscapes of the Emirates share one trait: water – be it the Creek, the Gulf, or the Lagoon, a reassurance perhaps that the city is but a small part of this country.

One of the larger and more ornate of the UAE's mosques, the Jumeira Mosque guides the observer's eye to trace the lines of the dome upward to the pinnacle. Symbolically, this architectural encouragement is meant to lift one's eyes towards God.

The richness of the visual landscape of the urban centers of the UAE constantly changes with the light and with the completion of new buildings. Polished glass reflects adjacent buildings and colours in endless variations.

Tradition and progress have struck a happy balance. Secular, globally commercialized aspects of life in Abu Dhabi exist harmoniously with religious traditions and beliefs. Each day, residents and visitors alike are reminded of this when the calls to prayer echo in the skyscrapers of the cities: it is a peaceful and reassuring sound that rings poignantly upon the ears.

Careful to preserve elements of its rich architectural past, the UAE has built or reconstructed elegant minarets that rise above the palms. As evening call to prayer drifts over the oasis, such silhouettes feel timeless.

This modern scene shows camels on their way to the Friday races. Held at the Camel Racetrack with the Dubai skyline in the distance, it is another example of tradition continuing to exist alongside postmodern development in the Emirates.

The abundance of glass skyscrapers combined with year-long vibrant sunshine results in a myriad of fascinating reflections and distortions of the city's architecture.

For many Dubai residents, a method of transport from one side of the Creek to the other; for visitors, a cultural delight. Abras, the local version of water taxis, are the least expensive sightseeing tour in the city, and arguably one of the best.

Formerly a design with defensive purposes, the spiked door now serves as a reference to traditional architecture. This particular door at the Dubai Museum blends both old and new with its ancient spikes and newer brass fixtures. Such minute details mark the contrasts that are a function of lightning-quick development.

Transitional geographies always fascinate, none more so than the beautiful locations where the sea meets the land. The contrast between water and earth, each with its own textures, hues, reflections, and smells, rouses the imagination. The vast openness of the water begs us to dream about endless possibilities.

The United Arab Emirates is blessed with a grand 1,318 kilometers of coastline, some of it on the Gulf of Arabia and the remainder on the Gulf of Oman. In the south, sabkha (salt-flats) gently give way to the water; in the north and east, golden beaches welcome the water and black mountains proudly rise out of the sea. With a myriad of blues and greens, salty waters splash colour into any seascape. Coasts provide a place to reflect upon the greatness of nature and remind us how insignificant we are by comparison. Extending to meet the horizon in the distance, great bodies of water have enchanted curious onlookers for millennia.

The history of Arabia has always involved the sea. As a means of transport, as a source of fish and pearls, and as an inspiration to dreams, the waters off the UAE remain a crucial component of cultural identity.

Perhaps there is an element of irony as well: in a land where fresh water has always been scarce, the sea historically must have seemed to taunt residents. Presently, enormous quantities of saltwater are processed in desalinization plants for use throughout the region; this resource has allowed the country to nurture plant life in the desert and transform entire landscapes into gorgeous green spaces.

On the west coast, the largely cloudless weather continually provides spectacular sunsets; on the east coast, the sunrises thrill. Either way, as the seasons change, so too do the colours and characteristics of the dawns and dusks. The light softens in the clear winter months whereas the glaring, harsh light of summers is often diffused by haze. This seasonal light paints seascapes in an ever-changing fashion such that the same physical scene rarely looks exactly the same.

Simply knowing that great bodies of water are near at hand may soothe us psychologically, but nothing can compare with making time to be awestruck on a regular basis. This tremendous resource resides near at hand: perhaps the following images can inspire a renewed excitement towards the stunning seascapes of the UAE.

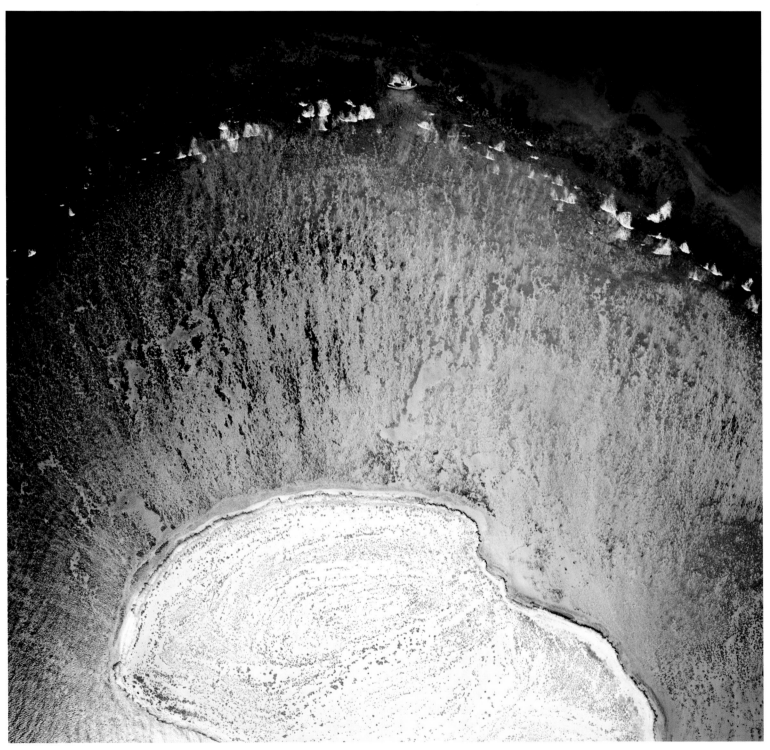

Many of the tidal islands and sandbars off Abu Dhabi's coast are popular afternoon destinations. Shallow water surrounding the island appears to have marooned an unlucky mariner. Although tides in the Gulf of Arabia rarely exceed one meter, in the shallow flats off much of the coast, this relatively small fluctuation in depth can force significant navigational changes.

Some wish to abandon the traditional ways in favour of modernity. A sturdy wooden dhow rests on
the sand at the end of the Dubai Creek, a reminder of the past.

A night dive off the east coast brings a plethora of visual rewards. A jellyfish hosting juvenile jacks floats past as many other species emerge in the safety of darkness to hunt and play.

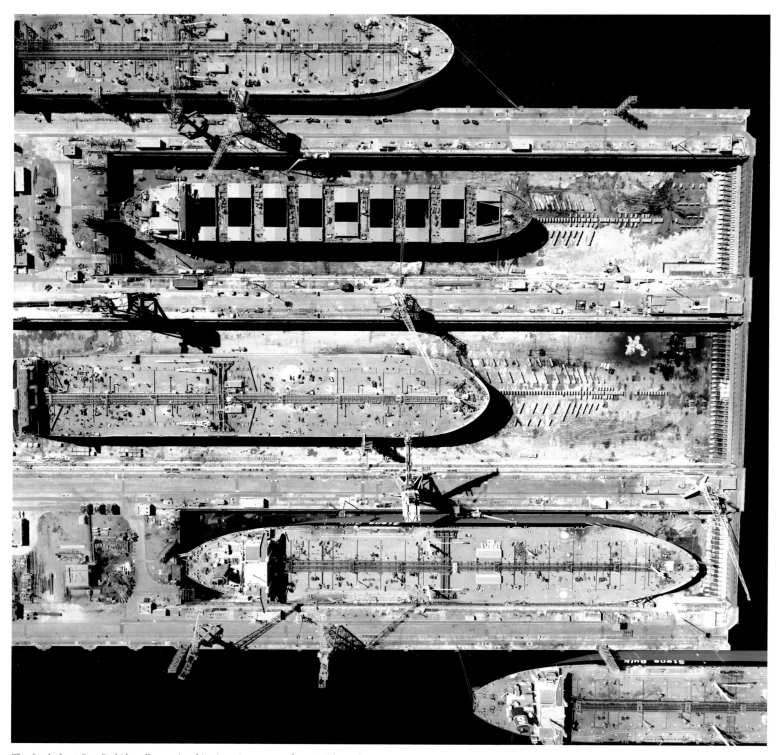

The dry docks at Port Rashid cradle massive ships in various stages of repair. The Dubai Dry Docks were an initiative of the late ruler of Dubai, Sheikh Rashid bin Saeed al Maktoum, in order to encourage shipping and trade in the region. One look at the ports of Dubai today will confirm the success of this initiative.

Whether natural or man made, everything in the Emirates is illuminated and tinted by abundant sunshine. The pace of growth and development in the Emirates defies imagination; machines and humans labour together to build this nation with blinding speed.

A dramatic finish to nearly every day, sunsets in the UAE consistently delight residents and visitors alike. Sometimes winds stretch wispy clouds across the twilight sky; at other times thick cloudbands refract the light into a vast smudge of orange on the horizon. In spite of the consistently clear weather, sunsets magically vary on a daily basis, especially in the winter months.

An irrigation channel - *falaj* in Arabic - delivers precious waters from a nearby underground spring. The result is a lush and fertile haven in an otherwise barren land. Largely found in plantations or farms, many falaj systems carry water for kilometers from source to field.

The light of the setting sun gently filters through the mists that rise in the canyons of Wadi Bih. At this time of day, shadows dominate the landscape, adding a softness to the sharp contours of the mountains.

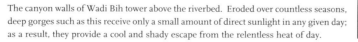

The canyon walls of Wadi Bih tower above the riverbed. Eroded over countless seasons, deep gorges such as this receive only a small amount of direct sunlight in any given day; as a result, they provide a cool and shady escape from the relentless heat of day.

A limited number of ancient buildings remain, but those that do are a pleasant reminder of the past. Bidiyah Mosque, the oldest in the UAE, with its massive buttresses and tiny round window - telltale features of traditional architecture - hails from 640 AD, and continues to retain a certain undeniable confidence.

As if defying the dunes to move any closer, a highway cuts through rippling red sands, and passes very near the famously high "Big Red" dune. Many travel this road in search of remote locations in which to partake in camping, dune bashing, and sand surfing - common weekend exploits in the UAE.

As nesting materials such as reeds and grasses are scarce, many species of birds improvise.
Here, sandstone cliff faces are riddled with small cave-nests; the thriving community of birds
testifies to the success of this tactic. With few natural predators in the region, approximately 240
species flourish - and consequently birdwatchers flock to the Emirates to observe and enjoy.

Stratified layers of sand in a dune near Shwaib demonstrate the slow but steady alterations of these ever-changing natural features. Without any vegetation to stabilize the sand, dunes are constantly eroded by wind and the rare rainfall. Cemented sands are the result of minerals such as calcium carbonate from ground water of a distant past's higher water table.

Crafty and opportunistic, the Sand Fox uses its acute senses to avoid danger and to hunt for food.
Though generally nocturnal, it is possible to catch a glimpse of a Sand Fox by day.

Where minimal ground cover exists, various creatures make themselves at home. A migratory Houbara nests in the grass, a temporary seasonal resident of the UAE.

Jebel Maleilah, more commonly known as 'Fossil Rock' stands at almost 400m above the surrounding dunes. The sand, rich with iron oxide, offers enthusiasts a fascinating insight into the natural history of the region as well as a particularly vivid and colourful landscape.

With one of the sunniest climates on earth and great stretches of beaches, no wonder the UAE finds itself immensely popular with holidaymakers. A lifeguard keeps watch over swimmers relaxing in the clean, blue-green waters of Jumeira.

On the coast, magnificent sunsets become a regular fixture in daily life. As the seasons change, the
weather remains fair, but the light changes from harsh and yellow in the summer months to softer
and more welcoming in the winter.

One of many fine hotels along the beach in Dubai, the Ritz-Carlton Jumeira lives up to its illustrious name. A perfect weekend escape as well as a destination resort, the hotel remains a favourite amongst residents and tourists alike. Slightly Mediterranean in feel, the Ritz-Carlton convincingly provides the illusion of being far far away from life's realities.

From high above, the magnitude of the Burj Al Arab complex becomes clear. Developers constructed a small island to serve as a foundation to the hotel, then built a curling breakwater – a thriving man-made "reef" for marine life – to shelter the harbour. The result is a significantly changed coastline and a bounty for those who wish to escape from it all without really leaving the city.

Fireworks often light up the Dubai skyline, especially during the annual Dubai Shopping Festival. As the nation grows and develops, the multicultural society that lives here will continue to marvel at the rapid pace of progress, and the fact that focus on enjoyment is never forgotten.

In souks, like that in Sharjah, antique jewelry and trinkets entice those with less flashy taste. Unique old pieces often come with fascinating stories that shop keepers readily offer over a cup of tea.

The world famous Gold Souk in Dubai overwhelms visitors with its glitter and its bargains. Display windows fairly overflow with gold and jewels, and sellers are eager to haggle.

Index
&
Acknowledgements